Original title:
Shaded Verses

Copyright © 2025 Creative Arts Management OÜ
All rights reserved.

Author: Victor Mercer
ISBN HARDBACK: 978-1-80567-348-4
ISBN PAPERBACK: 978-1-80567-647-8

## Lullabies of the Leafy Lane

In the garden where the dandelions dance,
A snail took a twirl, caught in a trance.
He slipped on a leaf, thought it was a bed,
Said, "Why rush, life's better when you play instead!"

The butterflies giggled, flitting about,
With jokes on their wings, there's never a drought.
One whispered, "Why did the tree wear a frown?"
The other just laughed, "Because it can't leaf town!"

Underneath an old oak, a frog made a throne,
Claimed himself king, with a crown made of bone.
The bugs all clapped wildly, started a cheer,
"A hop for the monarch! To us, he's a dear!"

In shadows where sunlight plays peekaboo,
A raccoon in pajamas stole some BBQ stew.
With sticky fingers, he waved as he fled,
"Come back, if you want, but heed what I said!"

So together they laughed, all creatures entwined,
In the leafy lane where the silly unwind.
Life's too short for troubles, let's laugh 'til we drop,
With lullabies sung, in a world set to hop!

## Beneath the Hushed Leaves

Under the trees, where squirrels conspire,
Laughter erupts like a pie in the mire.
A raccoon in pajamas, oh what a sight,
Dancing with shadows, in soft moonlight.

Whispers of branches, a giggling breeze,
Tickling the branches, the birds join with ease.
Mice play charades, they scamper and glide,
While owls roll their eyes, with nowhere to hide.

## **Shadows of the Dusk**

In twilight's embrace, the shadows take flight,
A cat serenades, what a curious sight.
He strums on a leaf, his paws in a twist,
Like a rockstar at dusk, none can resist.

Bats wear their capes, all the new fashion,
Swirling in circles, a quirky passion.
Frogs in tuxedos begin to perform,
A concert of croaks, both silly and warm.

## Verses in the Gloaming

The gnomes have a party, with hats far too big,
They trip on their shoelaces, they jig and they dig.
Their dance has no rhythm, yet they don't care,
Chortling with joy, they leap through the air.

Fireflies like lanterns, glow in a row,
While frogs with their crowns, put on a show.
Mice wear sequined jackets, strutting with pride,
In the realm of the gloaming, where laughter won't hide.

## Phrases in the Penumbra

In the penumbra, where whispers collide,
A snail writes a novel, with great sense of pride.
He types with his foot, oh what a sight,
As crickets recite, with all of their might.

A hedgehog recycles old jokes from the past,
While turtles debate who's the fastest at last.
In the dusk of the evening, humor takes flight,
As all critters gather, for fun and delight.

## Tales of the Tranquil Thicket

In the woods where squirrels play,
A bear wears shades on a sunny day,
Mice dance jigs on mushrooms tall,
While owls hoot at a squirrel's fall.

A rabbit's hat steals every show,
Raccoons trade secrets right below,
The grass sings soft with a tickle tune,
While frogs croak out a lively rune.

## Vignettes in the Veiled Corner

In a shadow where shadows sigh,
A lazy cat dreams as birds fly by,
With whispers of leaves that dive and spin,
A playful breeze tugs at every whim.

A gnome sneezes in a patch of moss,
While a hedgehog claims this spot as boss,
The fireflies flicker like tiny stars,
Telling tales of old, in the night, from afar.

## Colors of the Castle of Leaves

A castle made of vibrant green,
Where giggling fairies are often seen,
With leaf-made banners that flap with glee,
And crickets strum on a leaf guitar spree.

The flowers wear hats of every hue,
While butterflies gossip, it's all so true,
Bees buzz by with a clumsy grace,
As sunlight winks in a playful chase.

## Notes from the Nocturnal Nook

In a nook where night creatures dwell,
A raccoon sings songs under a shell,
With starlit eyes, they share a laugh,
As shadows dance on a tree trunk path.

An owl brings jokes, in woeful guise,
While fireflies spark like silly spies,
Bats may stumble but never frown,
The night wears laughter like a crown.

## **Chords of the Canopy**

In trees so tall, they wear a hat,
Squirrels dance, and chatty birds spat.
Leaves whisper jokes in the gentle breeze,
While ants march by with such elegance, please!

A raccoon laughs, trying to fit,
In the hole of a trunk, oh, what a hit!
The moon winks down, shining bright,
As shadows play tag, what a delight!

**Verses in the Veil**

Under the branches, the shadows prance,
Frogs in tuxedos join in the dance.
The sun peeks out, throws a silly grin,
A leaf on my head—where do I begin?

Bumblebees buzz with a comedic beat,
Wearing their stripes, they can't take the heat.
In the veil of dusk, the jokes never fail,
Laughter from crickets, a whimsical tale.

## Songs of the Shaded Hollow

In the hollow's heart, a turtle sings,
To a snail in a cap—oh, the joy it brings!
Fungi in tuxes hold a grand ball,
While a wise old owl droops in the hall.

With moonlit tunes, critters twirl,
A badger spins with a flurry and whirl.
In shadows and giggles, the night takes flight,
Under a starry quilt, everything's right!

# **Tones Woven in Twilight**

In twilight's glow, the shadows blend,
Beetles recite while the willows bend.
A skunk adds spice with a whoopee sound,
While fireflies twinkle, they dance all around.

The night is a tapestry of laughter spun,
With whispers of joy, and all things fun.
In croaking choruses, the night birds tease,
In the twilight's embrace, it's a breeze to please!

## Rhyme Brought by the Breeze

A squirrel wore a tiny hat,
He thought he looked quite debonair.
The breeze just laughed, said, 'Look at that!'
And blew his hat right in the air.

A rabbit danced a silly jig,
While birds became his backing crew.
They chirped and hopped, all kind of big,
As bunnies bloomed in blooms of dew.

The wind played tricks with every leaf,
Twirling them in a merry chase.
The trees just giggled, full of belief,
That laughter rang through every space.

The flowers joined the playful game,
In hues that brightened up the glen.
"Who needs a rule?" they cried with fame,
When whimsies rule the lives of men!

## Ponderings in the Gloom

A snail on stilts looked quite bemused,
As shadows danced around his shell.
He pondered, feeling somewhat used,
'Is gloom a place where jokes excel?'

With crickets chirping like a band,
He tapped his toes to playful tunes.
The fireflies lit up the land,
Creating sparkles like balloons.

One owl hooted with delight,
'Why worry when the night is here?
Just fly a kite, embrace the fright,
Let's find the joy in all we fear!'

Then grumpy mushrooms laughed aloud,
As ghoulish shadows flitted near.
In laughter thick, they formed a crowd,
And gloom was chased by cheerful cheer!

## Lyrics of the Leafy Labyrinth

In a maze of leaves, where secrets dwell,
   A hedgehog sang a curious tune.
  He sought a place where no one fell,
While humming under the watchful moon.

   A chubby raccoon stole his song,
  Claiming his tunes were quite the hit.
  But all the leaves just laughed along,
    As nature played her witty skit.

Then came a fox with rhymes to spare,
   Dancing wild with a twist and leap.
   He led the way with flair and flair,
  While critters gathered all to peep.

The berries burst with laughter bright,
As twirls and spins filled up the glen.
  In every turn, pure joy took flight,
    A leafy labyrinth of funny men!

## Fables from the Forest Floor

A tortoise told a tale so grand,
Of birds with shoes who flew real fast.
They wore each pair like a marching band,
And left the trees all in a blast.

A deer who painted with his nose,
Created stripes upon the bark.
'This artistry nobody knows,'
He claimed, 'but now my work's a spark!'

Amidst the fables, laughter soared,
While owls traded wisdom for glee.
With every story, joy restored,
They spun their tales by the old tree.

The forest floor became a stage,
For critters clad in funny skins.
In every fable bloomed the age,
Of laughter echoed in the winds!

## Rhapsody in the Roaming Shadows

In the park where shadows play,
Kids chase squirrels all night and day.
Laughter echoes, a joyful tease,
While dogs ponder their ancient dreams.

Sunbeams dance on the grass so bright,
While ants line up for a food delight.
Cats plot mischief from a high seat,
As the breeze carries whispers sweet.

Jumping jacks amidst the trees,
Mice do yoga with utmost ease.
Grasshoppers sing in a wobbly tune,
As shadows giggle beneath the moon.

So join the fun in this vibrant space,
Where light and dark share a playful chase.
Let your worries drift, take a break,
And embrace the silliness that shadows make.

## Debating the Dappled Dreams

In the forest where leaves disagree,
A squirrel claimed a nut for tea.
Frogs croak loudly, with pompous pride,
While beetles roll their eyes and hide.

Chirping crickets make their case,
While fireflies flash, lighting the space.
Branches argue, who wins the game,
Of who can bounce an acorn the same?

Rabbits hop in to join the chat,
Debating who's the fluffiest rat.
As sunshine rays spark up delight,
They all agree that jokes take flight.

So gather 'round this quirky scene,
Where every creature's a feisty teen.
With laughter as lively as a dream,
Life's a dance and shadows gleam.

## Queries in the Quietude

Beneath the boughs where whispers dwell,
A hamster ponders life quite well.
Does the sun glow brighter at noon?
Or is it just the smiling moon?

A tree asked the stone, quite perplexed,
"Do you ever feel so out of context?"
"Only when I roll down the hill,"
Replied the stone, quite full of thrill.

The wind chimed in with a breezy laugh,
"Yo, rocks don't roll—they just take a bath!"
Every twig had a thought to share,
Creating a chorus beyond compare.

So questions float in the gentle air,
While critters giggle without a care.
In this moment, a strange sort of bliss,
As shadows join in for a playful twist.

## Contrasts in the Cloistered Words

In the library where books reside,
A cat sat quiet, trying to hide.
While pages flapped with silent glee,
Daring each other to cause a spree.

A bookworm critiqued the ancient prose,
"Dear Squirrel, how's your nutty nose?"
While stories whispered of silly dreams,
Of dancing veggies and fruity creams.

The librarian shushed with a grin,
"But why must a potato wear a grin?"
Laughter erupted under her stare,
As children giggled and joined the flair.

In shadows cast by tales so absurd,
Words flipped and flopped, as they occurred.
Each contrast sparked such wild delight,
In this hoot of a gathering night.

## Flourish of the Faint Sun

A timid sun peeks from the leaves,
It tickles the ground and gently weaves.
The flowers chuckle, their petals in glee,
As they dance to the tune of a soft bumblebee.

The shadows stretch long, a playful disguise,
Where squirrels plot mischief with twinkling eyes.
They leap and they bound, a circus of cheer,
Laughing at clouds that drift ever near.

A garden of giggles, of whispers and fun,
Where every small creature plays under the run.
With sunshine so faint, yet waking the day,
In this funny realm, we all come to play!

**Narratives in the Nurturing Shade**

Under the boughs, stories unwind,
Of ants in a train, so perfectly blind.
They march with a purpose, a bustling parade,
While a lazy old turtle just takes shade.

The chirping of crickets, they plot and they scheme,
Trading wild tales like a whimsical dream.
A frog croaks a ballad, the crowd starts to sway,
In the nurturing coolness, they frolic and play.

A breeze comes to giggle, tousling some hair,
As fruits drop with laughter, light as the air.
The scene is a tapestry, woven with fun,
In a world where all stories are brightened by sun.

## The Quiet Lattice of Language

Whispers of words float on a breeze,
Like bees with their honey, they buzz with ease.
A shadow of laughter hangs in the air,
As the roots exchange tales, with a dash of flair.

The crickets are poets, their verses ignite,
In a lattice of silence, they dance in delight.
A sunflower turns, to hear the sweet tune,
As laughter and language harmonize soon.

A squirrel jots notes from a tree overhead,
Crafting a story before it's even said.
In this quiet embrace, the words take their flight,
As we giggle and ponder till day turns to night.

## Drapes of the Dreamy Tangent

In a land where the dreamers cast shadows so wide,
They wear hats made of clouds and take snails for a ride.
The grass giggles softly, a tickle of green,
While daisies whisper whispers, serene yet obscene.

A breeze brings a riddle, so sly and so cheeky,
It dances on toes of those feeling freaky.
The sun plays hide and seek, what a silly game,
As peacocks strut by, full of flaunt and of fame.

Each drape of the tangent holds secrets and glee,
For every odd wanderer still longs to be free.
In this realm of the joyful, where nonsense is king,
We frolic and laugh, as the wild zephyrs sing.

## Melodies of the Misty Meadow

In the meadow, cows wear shades,
They dance in circles, making trades.
The grass sings tunes, so very bright,
As butterflies take off in flight.

A rabbit hops, with style and flair,
He flips and flops, without a care.
The daisies giggle, tickled by breeze,
While a squirrel juggles acorns with ease.

A hungry frog croaks out a beat,
While ladybugs march with tiny feet.
All nature joins in this merry song,
In the misty meadow, where all belong.

With laughter laced in every tune,
The sun peeks out, as if to swoon.
In the woods, fun knows no end,
Where shadows dance and giggles blend.

## Letters from the Lush Labyrinth

In a maze of leaves, I wrote a note,
To a lost sock, which stayed afloat.
It replied with tales of grassy quests,
And escapades with mushroom pests.

I sent it off via a swift bluebird,
Who flapped away, not saying a word.
But a worm spoke back with a wiggle and grin,
Said my letter was found - buried within.

Next came a snail with a shiny shell,
Claiming secrets of the mossy dell.
He spoke of tea with a toad on a log,
And declared himself the king of the fog.

The letters flowed, like streams of fun,
From the labyrinth where mischief's begun.
Each word a chuckle, a twist, a tease,
In the lush of the trees, where laughter's a breeze.

## Whims of the Wildwood

In the wildwood, folks wear hats,
Made of twigs, adorned with rats.
They sip on dew from acorn cups,
And giggle loud, as laughter erupts.

A fox with shoes taps on the ground,
While owls spin tales, profound yet round.
The pine trees sway to a ragtime beat,
As chipmunks dance on their tiny feet.

An old bear croons a lullaby soft,
While the bees buzz around, taking off.
A ladybug winks with a mischievous eye,
In this realm where silliness flies high.

With joy at every turn and twist,
The wildwood's charm is hard to resist.
In shady glades, fun takes its course,
With whimsy and wonder, nature's true force.

## Canvases of the Clandestine

Under the leaves, artists create,
Funny creatures with odd traits.
A cat with shoes, a dog with a tie,
In the clandestine, talent won't die.

A hedgehog brushes, a porcupine sings,
Creating laughter as joy takes wings.
With paint made of berries and petals bright,
The night comes alive in this playful light.

A canvas of laughter, painted in cheer,
Where squirrels serve popcorn and dance with a deer.
They giggle and spin, creating a scene,
In the whimsical world of the unseen.

As shadows play tricks and moonbeams reflect,
Every corner holds joy to collect.
In the clandestine, where humor intertwines,
Life's colorful tapestry endlessly shines.

## Murmurs of the Moss

In the forest, mosses giggle,
Whispering secrets with each wiggle.
They wear tiny hats, all green and sly,
Plotting pranks as clouds float by.

Fungi join in, dance with glee,
A fungal fiesta, wild and free.
They chuckle at branches that trip on their toes,
While ants parade in their fancy clothes.

## Stanzas of the Subtle Breeze

The breeze flirts with hats, plays a game,
Swirling and twirling, oh what a fame!
It teases the trees, who laugh and sway,
"Catch us if you can!" the branches say.

Whispers of grass tickle the feet,
As breeze-borne giggles echo and meet.
A bumblebee mumbles, caught in between,
Chasing pollen dreams, oh what a scene!

## Secrets Among the Branches

Branches hold meetings, they gossip and grin,
Discussing the squirrel who once tried to spin.
"Did you see him fall?" a twig calls out loud,
"Guess acorn acrobatics aren't for the proud!"

Leaves share tales of the rain's funny dance,
How puddles formed in a slippery chance.
While mockingbirds chuckle, perched oh so high,
Singing silly songs as the clouds drift by.

## Odes to the Overcast

Oh clouds, you're a blanket, cozy but gray,
You hide from the sun, what a cheeky display!
As you block the bright, we giggle and tease,
'Make way for the moon' is the mantra of these.

Raindrops play tag, splashing with glee,
"Catch us if you can!" they roar with a spree.
With puddles as mirrors, we stomp and we cheer,
Finding joy in the gloom, never fear!

## Reflecting on the Restful Recess

In the park where shadows play,
Laughter dances, bright and gay.
Squirrels plot with sneaky eyes,
Chasing crumbs and wild goodbyes.

Swinging high, we touch the sky,
Feet like rockets, oh so spry.
Teachers frown, they try to hush,
But giggles rise in joyous rush.

Tugging hats, a silly show,
Chasing friends, we run below.
Jumping puddles, splashes fly,
Wet socks make us laugh and sigh.

## Takes on the Tamed Wilderness

In the woods, we seek our thrill,
With a map, we climb each hill.
Bears wear hats, they wave hello,
As we fumble, trip, and go.

An owl hoots out a silly cheer,
Telling secrets for all to hear.
Fireflies blink a catchy tune,
While we dance beneath the moon.

Raccoons rob our lunch with glee,
While we shout, "Hey, that's for me!"
Nature's pets have taken note,
Stealing snacks from our small boat.

## Wisps of the Windy Whisper

The breeze giggles as it flows,
Tickling leaves, a game of prose.
Kites are launched with roars and shouts,
As clouds puff up with silly doubts.

Jumping high, we chase the breeze,
Whisper secrets through the trees.
A squirrel joins our flying song,
Twisting, turning all day long.

Frisbees swirl, collide, and flop,
Wild shouts take us near the top.
Winds that whirl and giggle tight,
Make our day pure, pure delight.

## Mists of the Muted Muse

In the haze, where dreams entwine,
We sip cocoa, feeling fine.
Mugs like clouds in cozy hands,
As we weave our fanciful plans.

Fog descends with a playful wink,
Makes us giggle as we think.
A cat, a ghost, or maybe both,
Join our tales with playful oaths.

In this mist, we drift and sway,
Finding treasure in our play.
Let's get lost, then laugh it through,
For the sights are never few.

## Lines Woven in Gloom's Embrace.

In a corner where shadows play,
A jester's hat begins to sway.
His jokes are old, his shoes are bright,
He tumbled down, what a silly sight!

With giggles that echo in the air,
He slips on frown, but doesn't care.
A pie in hand, he takes his aim,
Watch out, the custard comes with fame!

His laughter dances with delight,
Beneath a moon so round and bright.
He juggles puns, they fly like birds,
Who knew gloom had such funny words?

So let's toast to the clownish flair,
For humor blooms in the thickest air.
In every dark, a spark ignites,
In shadows too, the joy invites!

## Whispers in the Twilight

In twilight's glow, the lights are green,
A raccoon dons a funny sheen.
He wears a tie, it's far too tight,
And scurries off in the fading light.

The owl hoots with a subtle grace,
As squirrels join to dance and race.
They drop acorns, what a mess!
In moonlit glee, they all confess!

"Who needs nuts when we can play?"
Cried out the critter leading the way.
With every leap, the laughter grows,
In shadows' grip, comedy flows!

So as the stars peek from afar,
They twinkle bright, the guiding star.
For in the dusk, where antics blend,
Life's silly side we must defend!

## **Echoes Beneath the Canopy**

Beneath the trees, a frog croaks loud,
He jumps in style, oh what a crowd!
His tiny hat is a sight to behold,
A prince in disguise, so brave and bold.

The critters laugh as he takes a dive,
In puddles deep where they all thrive.
"Not a royal, just amphibious fun!"
With splashes, he claims he's number one!

A turtle slow, with a wink so sly,
Challenged the frog, "Come take a try!"
With scrambled limbs, they race away,
As summer skies turn shades of gray.

Echoes of laughter fill the air,
Beneath the canopy, worries laid bare.
In ponds where whimsy reigns supreme,
Dreams float high in a funny dream.

## Ink Beneath the Arbor

A quill in hand, with ink so splashy,
A writer winks, his thoughts all trashy.
He scribbles tales of cats in hats,
And dogs who dance with acrobats.

Under the tree, his muse appears,
In scribbles bright, he conquers fears.
"Dear paper, let's take a silly twist,
For a laugh is what my heart insists!"

The wind it snickers, the leaves all chime,
With every stroke, he breaks from rhyme.
"Who needs structure, give me cheer!
I'll write my joy, so loud and clear!"

So ink takes flight, in shapes so bold,
With every drop, a story told.
Beneath the arbor, creativity flows,
In each funny line, hilarity grows!

## Whispers in the Half-Light

In the glow of a lazy sun,
Squirrels plot their mischievous run.
Sneaky shadows dance about,
While the world just laughs and shouts.

Lawn gnomes gossip, but who can tell?
They scheme and dream, oh what the hell!
A cat rolls by with a purr and a grin,
Thinking all this mischief is a win-win.

The breeze tosses leaves in the air,
Now a hat's gone, but do they care?
Friends gather round for a little tease,
In this half-light, laughter's a breeze.

So, let the jokes tumble and fall,
Under the trees where we all recall,
Life's a picnic of whimsy and cheer,
Wrapped in the funny, it's always near.

## Secrets Beneath the Canopy

Beneath the leaves where the squirrels play,
A secret life steals the breath away.
A frog in a tux gives a croaky bow,
To a passing bird who wonders how.

The ants march along in a funny line,
Each with a crumb, feeling just fine.
They stumble and bumble, it's such a sight,
On missions so grand but with zero flight.

A beetle brags of his shiny head,
While whispers of mischief spiraled and sped.
The shadowed stories tickle the ground,
Where giggles of nature can be found.

So come and laugh in this leafy hall,
Where secrets dance and shadows sprawl.
The forest is bursting with giggles and cheer,
In this silly world, joy's crystal clear.

## Silhouettes of Silence

Silhouettes loom in the fading sun,
While shadows whisper, 'Let's have some fun.'
A dog strikes a pose for an audience fake,
As crickets laugh hard, they start to shake.

The trees sway low in a borrowed scene,
Crack jokes about what they might have seen.
An owl hoots loud at a terrible pun,
But the night laughs back; it's not yet done.

Mice in tuxedos scamper and slide,
Under the twinkling stars, they collide.
The moon grins wide, a cheeky old friend,
Watching the antics that never quite end.

Under the cover of whimsical night,
These silhouettes bubble with pure delight.
In the hush of the dark, laughter ignites,
A comedy show under twinkling lights.

## Echoes in the Twilight

In twilight's glow, a llama prances,
Its humor tickles, causing glances.
The fireflies wink with a spark in their flight,
As the world shifts from day into night.

A hedgehog looks dapper in a tiny hat,
While the moon tries to dance, but slips on a mat.
The giggles are gaining, the scene's set in motion,
With echoes of laughter that start with devotion.

A raccoon shares tales of old hickory trees,
His fans are the owls and one buzzing bee.
The sky blushes pink as the jokes unfold,
In this vibrant hour, pure laughter is gold.

Come join the revelry, let's lift up our cheer,
For twilight's a friend, always near and dear.
Together we cherish this magical scene,
Where echoes of joy reign supreme.

## Poems from the Understory

In the layers just below,
Where light and laughter blend,
A squirrel steals my sandwich,
He considers me a friend.

The mushrooms giggle shyly,
As snails race on their trails,
Who'd guess that they're so speedy,
With tiny, slippery sails?

In shadows, the frogs sing tunes,
With crickets clapping hands,
While leaves dance to the rhythm,
In their leafy, green bands.

The tree roots hold vast secrets,
And hiccup as they grow,
Each twist tells a funny story,
That only the foxes know.

# The Calm in the Canopy

Up above the world so high,
The birds share rumors of the sky,
A parrot squawks, 'Did you hear?
The sun's wearing a hat! How queer!'

A sloth is snoozing with great flair,
While monkeys play truth or dare,
The breeze sends whispers through the leaves,
Of monkey tricks that no one believes.

Chubby raccoons in a conga line,
Decide to stop and sip some wine,
While squirrels chortle at their game,
Oh, trees have never been the same!

The dances high in verdant space,
Bring laughter to this leafy place,
So if you hear them sing and cheer,
Just know that it's the best time of year!

## Riddles in the Swaying Boughs

What's furry, sneaky, and chomps a snack?
The answer's simple: it's a raccoon attack!
Their jokes are cheesy, their antics loud,
They'll steal your picnic, then look so proud.

In the leafy realm of fun and games,
The whispers play their silly names,
The owls wink as they hoot and holler,
And all the squirrels just want to collar.

A riddle floats down like a feather,
'Why do trees always stay together?'
Because they've rooted in the fun,
And leaf it all to everyone!

So sway with me in this funny dance,
Where laughter lives and leaves take a chance,
To turn a frown into a smile,
And linger here for quite a while.

## Harmonies of Hidden Realms

In the nooks where secrets hide,
A hedgehog jigs with proud delight,
It spins around and trips a gnome,
Who shrieks, 'I'm late for tea at home!'

Elves strum banjos in the roots,
While pixies wear their tiny boots,
A crow steals socks from washing lines,
And all the folk just laugh and dine.

The cabbage patch joins in the fun,
With veggies dancing in the sun,
'Why is a carrot like a joke?'
It's all about the punch and poke!

So wander through these shaded lanes,
Where laughter bubbles and joy remains,
With every step, a giggle grows,
In this land, silliness flows.

## Echoing Elegies in the Evening

In the twilight, squirrels debate,
Who stole the nuts? Oh, what a fate!
A raccoon laughs, with a sly little glance,
While fireflies perform their glowing dance.

The owls hoot, claiming night's delight,
Though they all know, they sleep till bright.
Bats scatter, in their nightly spree,
A fuzzy brigade of chaos and glee.

Crickets chirp in a rhythmic beat,
As frogs jump in time, oh, what a feat!
The stars blink down, enjoying the show,
While the moon watches, amused, from aglow.

They echo in laughter, the evening sings,
Of mishaps and joys, oh what joy it brings.
While shadows play tricks in the fading light,
A concert of echoes, a comedic night.

**Dances in the Dappled Light**

Under the trees, how the shadows play,
A chicken joins in, hip-hopping away!
The sunbeams giggle, tickling the ground,
While the butterflies twirl, round and round.

In the meadow, grass sways to the beat,
As ants join the dance, small but sweet.
The daisies sway, waving their heads,
While a rogue breeze naps in their beds.

A rabbit spins, with a fluffy tail flair,
As the wind trips over, causing a scare.
The sun dips low, giving a nod,
To the merry brigade, a whimsical odd.

At dusk, they bow, what a sight to see!
The laughter of nature, wild and free.
With the last glimpse of light, they bid adieu,
In dappled dreams, the night will ensue.

## Portraits of the Pensive Shade

In the park, shadows wear funky hats,
While pondering life like wise old cats.
A sunbeam stops, curious at best,
"Hey, why so serious? Come take a rest!"

The wilting daisies proclaim their woes,
While mice in coats discuss fashion shows.
The trees lean in, eavesdropping unseen,
With leaves twitching, oh what a scene!

A lazy dog yawns, crown of dandelions,
Dreaming of tennis balls, oh what visions!
"Trust me," he sighs, "the world's a grand play,
Just dodge the cats, and you'll be okay!"

With chuckles exchanged, the shadows all jest,
In portraits of silliness, they're truly blessed.
For who knew life held such wondrous sights,
When pondering truth in the waning lights?

## Chants of the Quiet Grove

In the grove, a chorus of giggles bloom,
As leaves whisper secrets among the gloom.
A toad croaks a joke, old but clever,
As pinecones roll, their laughter a treasure.

The shadows dance, lured by a breeze,
Flirting with flowers, they sway with ease.
An old tortoise nods, wise and slow,
"Join the fun, take a chance, let's go!"

A rabbit twirls, showing off his tricks,
While critters gather, all in the mix.
Though night grows close, they're not feeling shy,
For in this grove, laughter will never die.

With the moon's gentle glow, they chant and play,
In their own funny way, they greet the day.
The chants echo softly, under starlit skies,
In a grove rich with chuckles and sweet lullabies.

**Lyrical Understory**

Beneath the leaves, the squirrels play,
Chasing shadows, bright as day.
A whispering breeze, a sneaky cat,
Contemplates who'll win this spat.

With giggles soft and laughter loud,
The daisies dance, a cheerful crowd.
While worms debate the best sunbeams,
Nature sprawls in silly dreams.

Tiny ants throw a picnic bait,
But the crumbs are far too great!
A line forms up, they march in pride,
Only to find their snacks have died!

In the corner, a funny frog,
Croaks a tune, like a dancing log.
His tongue flicks out, a grand buffet,
For passing flies who've lost their way.

# Hues of the Hidden Dawn

When morning comes, oh what a sight,
The toaster burns, it's quite a fright.
A coffee spill on yesterday's news,
I laugh it off, just old raccoon's blues.

In pajamas stained, I greet the morn,
With mismatched socks, my fashion is worn.
The cat gives me a judging stare,
As I trip over shoes, unaware!

The sun peeks through with a wink so sly,
While I undertake the pancake high.
My pancake flips are more like leaps,
Land on the floor, my breakfast weeps!

Yet there's a joy in such a plight,
As syrup cascades in morning light.
I smirk and dance amid the mess,
In this old kitchen, I am the best!

## Silhouettes of Sound

The night is here, the owls take flight,
A rumble comes, is it thunder or fright?
The wind's a-whistling a silly tune,
While mice hold a concert under the moon.

With squeaks and chirps, they form a band,
A cacophony, yet oh so grand.
The moonlight twinkles, a spotlight shown,
On a badger who prefers to moan.

Beneath the stars, the critters cheer,
One raccoon starts a funny leer.
He juggles nuts with utmost flair,
Until they rain down, everywhere!

In this rustic show, the laughter rolls,
Filling the woods with vibrant souls.
As dawn peeks in, the music wanes,
But echoes remain of silly refrains.

## Reflections in the Shade

Under the boughs, the shadows play,
With giggles that chase the gloom away.
A game of tag with sunlight's gleam,
Whisking giggles, a sunlit dream.

Frogs take notes from a wise old bee,
Discussing the art of the sandwich spree.
While snails debate, oh what a mess,
Who's the fastest? You'd never guess!

A grumpy old turtle joins the fray,
But naps defeat him, what a day!
With every laugh, the sun dips low,
In this lively patch, where wild things glow.

So come and sit in this lush retreat,
Where shadows dance and hearts skip a beat.
Embrace the charm, let worries fade,
In this sunny nook, where life's a parade!

## Inked in Dimness

In the dark, my pen did tumble,
All my words began to fumble.
I wrote a joke about a cat,
But it turned into a bat.

My sketches looked like Christmas trees,
With alien squirrels in the breeze.
I laughed so hard, I dropped my pen,
Now all my jokes are chalk and zen.

This ink I've spilled, it's quite a mess,
Like a salad in my Sunday dress.
I giggled as it turned to slime,
My masterpiece, a waste of time.

But still I cherish every line,
Each silly quip, a moment fine.
For in this gloom, laughter's bright,
Even in dimness, there's delight.

## **Lyrical Hues of History**

Historically, I tried to rhyme,
About a chicken, quite sublime.
She crossed the road to find a beat,
But lost her way to a disco treat.

In dusty scrolls, I penned her tale,
But added ants that danced in gale.
They jived along with medieval flair,
While knights applauded from their chairs.

Once a bard, now a jester's muse,
With every line, I'd rather snooze.
Yet here I prance, a poet's plight,
In silly shoes, by candlelight.

So raise a glass to times long past,
With giggles and hiccups, we'll amass.
For history's a grand parade,
Where laughter's hues shall never fade.

## The Palette of Dusk

At dusk, my paintbrush took a dive,
It swirled and twirled, alive, alive!
A purple pickle danced with glee,
While licorice clouds brewed sugary tea.

I splattered colors, bright and wild,
Each stroke like that of a cheerful child.
A moonlit cupcake tried to trot,
Leaving frosting trails in the plot.

Doves wore hats of spun cotton candy,
While bunnies juggled, oh so dandy!
The canvas giggled, had a fit,
As I painted on, a dandy wit.

So in this dusk, I'll laugh and tease,
With colors bending on the breeze.
For every splash, a wink and cheer,
The palette glows, let's draw near!

## **Beyond the Glistening Glade**

In the glade where fireflies sing,
I tripped on roots, oh what a thing!
I swore I'd bag a poem tonight,
But instead I sparked a moth fight.

Around the trees, the laughter chased,
As squirrels in hats showed off their taste.
One pulled my shoelace, oh what a laugh,
Then promptly posed for a photo graph.

The moon sent down a gentle wink,
As I contemplated, did I stink?
But here in jest, I'd rather be,
In this merry woods, wild and free.

So grab your quirks and dance tonight,
Embrace the giggles, hold on tight.
For in this glade, full of delight,
Even mishaps turn out right.

## Beneath the Leaves of Longing

Beneath the trees, we play hide and seek,
The squirrels are watching, oh how they sneak!
A whispered secret, a giggle escapes,
While pigeons above wear their funny capes.

The shadows dance, they wiggle and sway,
A leaf fell down and stole my toupee!
With branches laughing, the sun starts to tease,
As I chase a butterfly, stumbling with ease.

Yet there's a picnic, sandwiches and fries,
Ants march like soldiers, oh what a surprise!
"Hey, they're taking over!" I shout with a grin,
But they're just here for crumbs, let the party begin!

Among the laughter, beneath the green crown,
We build our castle of leaves, not of brown.
With sunlight peeking through gaps oh so small,
Who knew fun could grow down and not just from tall?

## Tints of Twilight Transactions

In the dusk, we barter with shadows and light,
Trading our giggles for starry delight.
A firefly flickers, "Hey, that's not a deal!"
I offer him candy; he says, "Let's just squeal!"

The moon wears a grin, a hilarious sight,
It winks at the sun, who's off for the night.
As owls hoot gossip with an echoing flair,
Their jokes are so bad, we can't help but stare.

We share silly stories about lost tennis shoes,
And the dog that tried dancing but only confused.
With whispers of twilight, we laugh 'til we snort,
Who knew the dark could support such a sport?

In a world of giggles painted dusk's lovely hues,
Every shade of laughter, we can't refuse.
So grab me a glowworm, my friend, let's not wait,
To dance in the twilight, it's never too late!

## Whispered Stanzas in the Grove

In our grove where the trees play dress-up in cheer,
We scribble our verses, no worries, no fear.
The grass shakes with laughter as we share our best line,
While crickets keep time, "Oh, you'll be divine!"

A frog jumped in, croaking puns all around,
"I'm totally ribbiting!" what a sound!
With daisies as our crowns, we write without pause,
Ensuring each stanza is worthy of applause.

A squirrel chimes in, bringing berries for snacks,
"Here, the sweetest treat, get ready for laughs!"
We gather our treasures, with jokes on repeat,
The carefree atmosphere can't be beat.

Among whispered verses, the grove lives and sings,
With puns on the branches and joy in the wings.
A place where giggles turn into pure art,
With every soft murmur, we're filling the heart.

## Murmurs of the Mottled World

In a world where colors blend, twist, and twirl,
We find hidden gems in the chaos that swirls.
A butterfly giggles, "I'm just here for the cake!"
While daisies roll their eyes, "For goodness' sake!"

The sun pokes around, with its peachy bright face,
"Caught you in laughter, what a glorious place!"
As the shadows shuffle, they start up a beat,
With whispers of rhythm, we dance on our feet.

With every odd creature that waddles or hops,
We join in their jests until laughter just plops.
A skunk tells a story, and we're all holding breath,
"Is it funny or stinky?" but we love it the best!

In this mottled world where the oddest is king,
We thrive on the humor that nature can bring.
So join in the murmurs, let your heart feel the glee,
For laughter's the treasure, let it set us all free!

## Harmony in Half-Light

In the glow where shadows play,
A cat sings jazz at the end of the day.
The mice tap dance, quite unaware,
Of the whiskered maestro's funky flair.

A lamp flickers, sparks ignite,
As roaches gather for a late-night bite.
They waltz on crumbs, a gourmet spread,
While the dog dreams of bacon in bed.

Moonlight drips like honey run,
A pool of giggles beneath the sun.
In this twilight, all seems absurd,
And laughter's the sweetest, silliest word.

So here we dance through half-light's sweep,
With dreams as wild as the prancing sheep.
In our hearts, we'll keep a tune,
While gnomes do the cha-cha under the moon.

## Syllables of the Serene

Whispers flutter in the breeze,
While squirrels argue over their cheese.
A zen garden with a quirky spin,
Where rakes are swords in a playful din.

Bamboo sways with a gentle tease,
As otters giggle in the trees.
They juggle stones with perfect grace,
In this odd, serene little space.

Harmonious shouts from a frog so bold,
Claiming the pond with his tales of old.
His voice echoes, a comedic sound,
As fish snicker quietly, huddled around.

In this realm where oddballs dwell,
Life's a joke, and we laugh as well.
With syllables spun from the clouds above,
We find that joy's the strangest love.

## Musings of the Marginal Sun

A sunbeam peeks from behind a cloud,
Tickling trees, oh isn't it loud!
With smiles stretching step by step,
In the warmth where the shadows prep.

Chickens cluck in a banter spree,
Debating the best way to be free.
While a dog holds court with his prized bone,
Counting the laughs with a big, happy groan.

The grass whispers secrets to ants on a stroll,
While daisies giggle in the sun's gentle roll.
A lizard rebuts with a wink and a nod,
In this place where the day's a little odd.

So we ponder laughter in the golden hue,
Where every glance brings something new.
In the light where joy takes flight,
We find musings in the marginal light.

## Renditions of the Rain-Softened Ground

Puddles reflect the world upside down,
As raindrops compete for the biggest frown.
The ground's a canvas, a squishy delight,
Where boots make music in joyful flight.

A worm wiggles, performing a dance,
With a chorus of frogs cheering his chance.
The sun sneaks out, wiping tears from the sky,
As clouds burst forth with a glorious sigh.

Roses bloom with a splattering cheer,
Winking at raindrops in the atmosphere.
While puddles splash, the stories unfold,
As the earth giggles in hues bright and bold.

So let's make renditions of laughter and rain,
In the mud, we'll lose all our worry and pain.
With every giggle as the clouds drift apart,
We find joy lives in the soft, tender heart.

## Chronicles of the Concealed

In a world so tucked away,
Lies a cat that thinks it's a dog.
It barks like a pro all day,
While wearing its favorite frog.

Behind the couch, a spy we meet,
A mouse with a top hat and cane.
He dances on tiny little feet,
Escaping every time it rains.

The plants all giggle when they sway,
In a breeze that whispers a joke.
Their leaves turn red, then fade to gray,
Like a cover of mischief they cloak.

O'er the moonlight, shadows prance,
A squirrel dressed up as a knight.
It holds a peanut, in a stance,
That makes the owls blink in fright.

## **Whispered Wishes in the Wandering Green**

There's a frog with a golden crown,
Sipping tea from a lily pad.
He squawks, 'Time to jump up and down!'
While the dragonflies all seem sad.

A turtle races, slow but proud,
In a contest with a quickened breeze.
The spectators all cheer aloud,
Noticing it's wearing two bees.

In hidden corners where squirrels meet,
A game of hide and seek unfolds.
Whoever trips over a beet,
Must wear a sock that's two sizes bold.

The flowers play pranks in the sun,
Hiding insects in blooming crests.
In this garden of laughter and fun,
Even weeds dress up in their best vests.

## Harmony of Hushed Handlings

Under branches where mischief sleeps,
A raccoon won't share his stash.
He giggles as the squirrel peeps,
Hoping to grab just one quick flash.

The shadows dance to a tune so light,
With whispers of laughter in the air.
Frogs croak out their feelings, just right,
Their crooning confuses all the hair.

Amidst the thicket, a rabbit sighs,
He's wearing someone's missing shoe.
Chasing dreams 'neath a starlit skies,
He hops and thumps, not caring what's true.

As day turns to night without a fuss,
The chirping crickets sing a joke.
Each note is wrapped in a spirited buzz,
Till even the moonlight starts to poke.

# Inscription in the Inverted Light

In a world where shadows play the fool,
A hedgehog writes with a quill of a twig.
It pens down secrets—don't be a tool,
While wearing a garland all bright and big.

An owl with spectacles, oh so wise,
Reads the gossip from a wrinkled leaf.
It hoots in ranges, and none despise,
Everlistening to laughter, but no grief.

Tomatoes roll away from the vine,
In hide-and-seek with sunlit glee.
While chasing shadows, they seem to shine,
Pretending they're fast as can be.

With giggles shared among the whirls,
As the stars giggle down from above,
The creatures play games, their joy unfurls,
In a nighttime broadcast of love.

## **Veiled Verses of the Forest**

In a forest where squirrels wear hats,
The owls giggle at all the spats.
Trees whisper secrets, quite absurd,
To the passing beetle, who plans to herd.

Mushrooms dance in their little shoes,
While rabbits debate about which is blues.
A fox tells jokes that are quite out of line,
Yet somehow, the deer think they're divine.

The brook bubbles over, with laughter it sings,
About the tall tales of magical things.
Fairies in pajamas share their delight,
As the moon joins the party, shining so bright.

And if you listen, in the dark hours,
You'll hear the night fox touching the flowers.
By morning they all melt away in the sun,
Leaving behind only laughter and fun.

## Shadows Breathing Word by Word

A shadow stretched under a wiggly tree,
Spilling out secrets, oh so carefree.
It whispers to bunnies as they hop along,
Crafting a story that's silly, not wrong.

The chipmunks gather, their story starts here,
Of a cat on a skateboard, oh what a cheer!
They giggle and grin, as they twist and shout,
Imagining journeys that leave them in doubt.

Moonlight winks as it plays hide-and-seek,
Shadows creating a game quite unique.
It stretches and yawns, then dances away,
Just before dawn steals the night's bright display.

Laughter cascades through the rustling leaves,
As each tale of woe, the forest believes.
A world spun of light, deliciously strange,
Where every dark corner invites a new change.

## Reflections in the Woodland Light

In the woodland where the fireflies glow,
A mouse tells of cheese disasters below.
He made a great trap, to catch a big snack,
But ended up caught, in a funny old sack.

The trees roll their trunks, they laugh out loud,
As a crow tries to sing, in front of the crowd.
Twigs join harmonies, leaves do the beat,
While the pond jumps in with ripples of heat.

Chirps of the crickets, a musical tease,
Scoff at the frogs, who croak just to please.
With every mishap, there's joy to be spun,
In this wacky little land where we all have fun.

With sunbeams aflutter, painted with glee,
Every shadowy nook is a sight to see.
So remember the tales that make nature bright,
Where laughter and joy are the true woodland light.

## The Poetry of Forgotten Glades

In glades where the wildflowers start to sway,
A snail recites poetry at the end of the day.
His verses are slow, but charmingly fun,
As he blends in with daisies, one by one.

A bear in the thicket plays hide-and-seek,
With a chipmunk who thinks he's quite sleek.
They tumble and roll, what a sight to behold,
Their antics brought forth, by stories retold.

Butterflies flutter, with rhymes in their wings,
Whispering dreams of fantastical things.
The trees sway and nod, keeping beat with the breeze,
While laughter erupts at the antics of bees.

In these forgotten glades, where the wild things hide,
Every little moment can turn the tide.
So share in the laughter, let your heart play,
For life is a poem, in its own silly way.

## Mystic Moments in the Mist

In the fog, we dance and play,
Bumping into ghosts of yesterday.
One laughed, said, 'I'm just a breeze!'
I replied, 'Well, hush! Just freeze!'

Misty monsters roam around,
Somehow always wearing brown.
A foghorn hoots, a sleepy snore,
'Are you lost?' 'No, just wanting more!'

Whispers wrap like scarves so tight,
Tickling tales from left to right.
The shadows giggle, quite absurd,
In this mist, who needs a word?

When morning breaks, with sunlight's beam,
We might wake up, to find it's a dream.
Yet we'll laugh, not have a clue,
If it's the mist or me and you!

## Sonnet of the Swaying Trees

Oh, the trees are having a ball,
Swinging limbs like a carnival call.
One branches out, then trips on a root,
Said, 'I meant to leap, not to scoot!'

They gossip soft in leafy tones,
Making jokes about the stones.
A squirrel chimes in with a pun,
'Why don't rocks ever go out for fun?'

Breezes tickle their bark so fair,
Rustling secrets, who needs a chair?
Watching clouds, they can't help but sway,
Pretending to dance, come what may.

By dusk they pose, in silhouettes,
Cracking laughs, dodging regrets.
With every gust, they're quite a sight,
What a time in the fading light!

## Artistry of the Aged Bark

The old oak wears wrinkles with pride,
Tales etched deep, it can't hide.
'Watch your step,' it groaned with glee,
'You don't want to trip on history!'

In knots and grooves, stories hide,
Of beavers who thought they could glide.
Tree rings spun like cosmic lace,
'Ever tried to dance with a vase?'

Moss paints accents like a brush,
As insects hear the evening hush.
With every creak, it tells a jest,
'This bark's not rough; it's just well-dressed!'

In twilight's glow, shadows blurt,
Of dreams once lost and scents of dirt.
What life, what laughter held so dear,
In each grain, a chuckle we hear.

## Lines of the Lantern Light

Beneath the glow of amber hue,
A fairy's hat, not one, but two!
They giggle, flicker, dance with flair,
'Careful now! You might get a scare!'

Lanterns swing and sway with dance,
Each shadow casts a quirky glance.
One whispered, 'Why don't ghosts glow bright?'
Another snorted, 'Too much fright!'

The path ahead is full of jig,
As stories leap and shadows dig.
A light that hops from here to there,
'Thank goodness for this lively air!'

So gather round, let mischief sprout,
In every flicker, laugh, and shout.
With each new glow, we see the night,
Finding whimsy in lantern light!

## **Lines in the Lattice of Light**

In a garden where the whispers play,
A squirrel steals the sun's warm ray.
He leaps and twirls with such delight,
   A furry acrobat taking flight.

The shadows giggle beneath the trees,
While flowers dance in the gentle breeze.
A light show blooms in the midday glow,
   As bees put on their buzzing show.

   A butterfly's in a silly chase,
With a bumblebee, what a funny race!
They zig and zag, no end in sight,
Under the sun, it feels just right.

So join the fun, forget your woes,
As nature's laughter brightly glows.
In this vibrant, silly scene,
Light and laughter reign supreme.

## Secrets of the Sun-Dappled Path

On a trail where shadows play hide and seek,
A rabbit hops with a little squeak.
He finds a hat that fell from a head,
And proudly wears it; what a thread!

Footsteps crunching on the way,
A dog pauses to join the fray.
Wagging a tail with such a charm,
He stumbles over a twig, oh alarm!

The dappled light makes patterns that tease,
As squirrels rehearse their leap with ease.
A sunbeam tickles a sleepy snail,
While laughter echoes in the gnarled trail.

So scamper along with a grin so wide,
In the giggles of nature, you can hide.
These secrets found on this vibrant way,
Will turn your frown to bright buffet.

## Braids of Light and Shade

Under the trees where shadows join hands,
A cat naps softly, dreaming of bands.
He twitches and purrs in a sunlit beam,
Chasing imaginary fish in a dream.

A dog appears with a comical prance,
Chasing shadows, thinking it's a dance.
He trips on the grass and lands with a thud,
Becomes best friends with the warm muddy mud.

The birds chirp a tune in playful jest,
As if they're declaring who's truly the best.
Ducks in the pond quack their own rap,
While the frogs croak in a synchronized clap.

So laugh with the light, embrace the shade,
In this world where giggles never fade.
Let the braids of joy twist your heart,
As nature's humor plays its part.

## The Quill of the Dusk

As the day becomes dusk, a poet sways,
With a feather quill, he scribbles away.
His thoughts chase fireflies, a glowing brigade,
While the moon winks fondly in the shade.

A cat jumps up, aiming for the sky,
And lands on his head with a tiny sigh.
The poet chuckles, adjusts his cap,
While penning each whimsical mishap.

The stars twinkle like mischief in flight,
With a loud hoot, an owl takes to the night.
A raccoon interrupts with a curious face,
Making the poet lose his place!

So as the dusk unfolds its soft tricks,
And laughter joins the evening mix.
Let the quill of twilight write in jest,
For every moment's a comical quest.

## **Veils of Dappled Dreams**

In a forest of giggles, where shadows play,
Trees wear hats made of sunlight ballet.
A squirrel recites with a nutty tone,
While mushrooms dance on their wobbly throne.

Frogs in tuxedos leap over the brook,
With eyes like saucers, they won't read a book.
The breeze tells secrets in a whispering laugh,
As fireflies joke on a night-time behalf.

The colors collide in a whimsical spree,
Where shadows wear sneakers and dance with glee.
Tickled by moonbeams in a raucous delight,
The veil of the night flirts with flickering light.

So join the parade, with a chuckle or two,
In dappled dreams where fun's never through.
The laughter resounds, a contagious affair,
In this carnival shade, joy hangs in the air.

## **Beneath the Arc of Shadows**

Underneath arches made by the trees,
Witty whispers dance in the teasing breeze.
A raccoon juggles acorns with pride,
While punny puns in the foliage hide.

The sun winks down with a playful grin,
As chirps of the crickets start a cacophonous din.
A turtle makes jokes, slow on its feet,
As laughter erupts from the colorful fleet.

Shadows play hopscotch, jumping with glee,
While nimble little shadows sip lemony tea.
The world is a stage, and laughter's the play,
As gnomes tip their hats in a jovial way.

The hour is silly, the mood's full of cheer,
Beneath the arc where fun doth appear.
So twirl in the light, lose track of the time,
For shadows are ages where the world feels sublime.

## The Language of Half-Tones

In the land of half-tones where giggles reside,
Colorful whispers and pandas collide.
A parrot tells tales with a peppery flair,
While monkeys mimic in a mismatched pair.

Hues of confusion paint clouds in a haze,
As colors converse in a puzzling craze.
Red tells a fib, blue laughs in retort,
While yellow plays chess in a sunny cohort.

Each tone has a joke, a humorous claim,
In a palette of giggles, none feels the same.
They frolic and jest in a merry charade,
Where shadows are jesters in laughter arrayed.

With every brushstroke, the humor expands,
As art plays a symphony with playful hands.
So join in the fun of this visual spree,
In the language of laughter, let your heart be free.

## Where Light Meets the Gloom

In a kingdom of contrasts, where light takes a leap,
Silly shadows giggle while the darkness peeks.
The sun plays tag with a mop-top of gray,
As leprechauns dance in a hilarious fray.

Clouds wear clumsy shoes, stumbling in pairs,
While laughter erupts from the light's funny flares.
Gloom tries to frown, but it tickles too much,
As the dance of the light gives darkness a touch.

A cat in a top hat juggles moonbeams bright,
With lightning bugs beaming in a comical flight.
The day and the night, in a playful embrace,
Swirl in an outcome of smiles on their face.

So twirl in the twilight, laugh loud in the gloom,
For where light and darkness together consume,
A party ignites, a delightful ruse,
Where giggles abound and shadows amuse.

## Poems From the Periphery

In the corners, shadows dance,
Lurking squirrels in a romance.
They plan heists for the acorn prize,
Conspiracies under open skies.

Nearby, a cat sneezes loud,
Startling birds from their proud crowd.
They flap and squawk, make a great fuss,
While the cat just rolls, says, "That's just us!"

Beneath the tree, I hear a quack,
A duck on the loose—not a thing to hold back!
It chases a frog, they tumble and flop,
Nature's own blooper reel—what a non-stop!

At dusk, the sun casts a goofy glow,
As neighbors pretend they don't know.
A dance-off starts with a couple of geese,
While squirrels judge, looking for peace.

## Verses of the Verdant Veil

Behind the leaves, a whisper calls,
Frogs with top hats, they plan the balls.
They waltz on lily pads, all so spry,
While dragonflies buzz, giving it a try.

A bunny hops, with style, no doubt,
Wearing shades, he struts about.
He trips on a root, does a little dance,
Catching the sun—oh, what a chance!

The grasshoppers cheer, a lively crew,
With each little jump, they break into two.
A picnic forms, crumbs fly in the air,
As ants march in, nibbles to share.

As twilight falls, laughter ignites,
Fireflies scatter with tiny lights.
In this secret world, silliness reigns,
Where joy is found, and no one complains.

## Adrift in the Dappled Dusk

In twilight's glow, a raccoon sneaks,
Searching for snacks, he truly peaks.
With paws a-flutter, he digs a hole,
What treasures found in this night stroll!

A shadow prances, it's just my shoe,
Oh wait, it's a fox who thinks so too!
A mirthful chase along the path,
Giggling at us, nature's own math.

A hedgehog grumbles, trying to nap,
As critters dance around, a lively trap.
He grunts and rolls, pools of laughter grow,
While a squirrel throws nuts—from up high, who knew?

Beneath the trees, the giggles rise,
As creatures bask in twilight skies.
In this playful realm where laughter swells,
Even the moon starts chuckling, oh well!

## Stories in the Silhouette Light

By the light of dusk, shadows unfold,
A turtle tells tales, so brave, so bold.
Wears a cape made of leaves, what a sight!
He swears he once soared, oh what a flight!

A crab comes into play, with a strut so grand,
Telling fish tales about his beach band.
With claws raised high, he steals the stage,
While jellyfish bob, taking up the rage.

Wily whispers rustle through the trees,
A woodpecker taps with rhythmic ease.
He drums up a story of how he flew,
Straight into a branch—oh, what a view!

At the end of the night, sprites come alive,
Swirling around in a jolly drive.
In the laughter of shadows, magic ignites,
As their stories mingle 'neath the starry lights.

## Sagas of the Sunken Garden

In a patch of green where the gnomes take naps,
The flowers gossip, trading old mishaps.
The carrots joke, 'We're the cool kids here!'
While the sunflowers dance, spreading cheer.

A squirrel stumbles, chasing a wayward nut,
He trips on a pebble, landing in a rut.
The daisies laugh, their petals in a whirl,
While the earthworms contemplate their twirl.

A dandy dandelion gives a loud sneeze,
Causing chaos among the buzzing bees.
They buzz and whirl, making quite a fuss,
As the hedgehog chuckles, 'Now that's a plus!'

In this quirky patch, where odd things bloom,
Laughter grows as freely as perfume.
Every laugh, a seed in the rich, dark earth,
In this sunken realm of joy and mirth.

## Thoughts Entwined in Tendrils

Vines twist and turn like a playful child,
Chasing after thoughts, though slightly wild.
They coil around wisdom, sipping like tea,
Turning riddles into laughter, carefree.

The mushrooms gather, with hats on their heads,
Telling tall tales as the evening spreads.
One claims to fly, another insists,
That they can whisper to clouds on a mist.

A ladybug joins with a wink and a nod,
Says, 'I'm the queen, and that's just the odd!'
The fireflies giggle, lighting up the night,
Creating a dance floor, all twinkling bright.

In this tangled garden, a circus unfolds,
With whimsical beasts and adventures bold.
Laughter entwines with the vines all around,
In a world where silliness knows no bound.

## Cadence of the Cloistered Night

When dusk falls down like a velvet cloak,
The moon bursts out with a wink and a joke.
Crickets begin their chirpy little song,
While the toads croak, saying, 'We can't be wrong!'

In the stillness, a raccoon sneaks a snack,
While the owls hoot, plotting a comical attack.
A brave little mouse, with courage so clear,
Challenged the shadows, saying, 'I'm not here!'

The constellations sizzle like stars with a grin,
Twinkling and giggling through thick and thin.
Peering down, they decree with delight,
'Let's turn this night into one full of light!'

In the cloak of the night, jests are set free,
As oddball creatures hum their symphony.
Laughter echoes where shadows collide,
In the whispering breeze where secrets reside.

## Imagery of the Interlaced Branches

Branches twist and twirl in a playful ballet,
Mocking the wind who tries to sway.
Leaves laugh together, wearing hue and shade,
While squirrels debate the best acorn trade.

A parrot squawks tales of old ancient lore,
While the sun slips away, quickly wanting more.
The shadows giggle, flitting from tree to tree,
As the trees curtsy, saying, 'Look at me!'

Breezes carry whispers from leaf to leaf,
Spreading laughter like a joyful motif.
Each rustle a chuckle, a soft, gentle hum,
In this vibrant place, they all come undone.

As moonlight paints patterns in silvery shades,
The creatures unite in a dance that cascades.
Fun intertwines like the branches above,
In this whimsical world, where all hearts shove.

www.ingramcontent.com/pod-product-compliance
Lightning Source LLC
Chambersburg PA
CBHW051651160426
43209CB00004B/868